All I Want
for Christmas

Opening the Gifts of God's Grace

LEADER GUIDE

James W. Moore's

All I Want
for Christmas

Opening the Gifts of God's Grace

John P. Gilbert

ALL I WANT FOR CHRISTMAS
Leader Guide
Copyright © 2016 by Abingdon Press
All rights reserved.

Scripture quotations unless noted otherwise are from the Common English Bible. Copyright © 2011 by the Common English Bible. All rights reserved. Used by permission. *www.CommonEnglishBible.com*.

ISBN: 9781501824227

16 17 18 19 20 21 22 23 24 25—10 9 8 7 6 5 4 3 2 1
MANUFACTURED IN THE UNITED STATES OF AMERICA

Contents

How to Lead This Study

Welcome!

You're going to lead an exciting Advent study. This Leader Guide contains important suggestions to help you lead, and this first section provides some general tips before you begin.

But first, a word about Advent.

Advent is not Christmas! Advent is a special holy time. It is a time of anticipation, of preparation, of watchfulness, and of waiting. It is a time of looking forward to what God is going to do, of recalling what God has done, and of discovering what God is doing right now in our very midst. Yes, we know that Christmas is coming on the calendar, but the mystery and wonder of God's presence in our lives makes us eager to learn what God has in store for us this year, this season, this very day.

Here are some "Nuts and Bolts" to help you start your study off right:

Promotion

That's not a bad word in church! Let folks know your congregation is planning this study. The church newsletter, the worship bulletin, posters on the bulletin boards, social media, and word of mouth are all ways to promote this study. A hint: Promote early enough so that you can have a "stand-up" meeting of participants so that all can agree on the best day and time to meet.

Group Size

Think in terms of "six-sixteen." Fewer than six participants often have a hard time making for a good, lively discussion every week. And if one or two people miss a meeting, your group will be really small. At the other end, sixteen group members are about the maximum for good discussion. Over sixteen interested in this study? Form two or three or more groups! (And don't feel you must lead them all.) Fewer than six folks interested? Consider checking with some neighboring churches; perhaps two or three churches could join together to have a study group—or several groups!

Session Duration

Aim for ninety-minute sessions. Start and end right on time. Even if everyone is not present, start on time—and keep faith with participants by ending on the agreed-upon time. But if folks want to linger after the session, that is fine.

Room Arrangement

Can you set up a square of tables for your group? Four six- or eight-foot tables arranged in an open square in the fellowship hall or other large space works well. That way, everyone can see and hear everyone else. A hint: You as the leader can sit at a different location for each session. That way there is no "head" of the group, and you become an active participant in the discussions. Another hint: Suggest that spouses not sit together. This enriches discussions, too, because you'll be talking in twos, threes, and fours sometimes—and spouses often already know each other's thoughts and opinions!

Refreshments?

Sure! After all, we're a church—"We meet; we eat!" But keep refreshments simple. A bowl of salty (nuts, pretzels, or similar items) and a bowl of sweet (such as small wrapped candy) on each table is all that's needed. These can be passed back and forth at each table. Something to drink? Put a coffee pot on or provide water. If folks want something else—soda, for example—have them bring their own. Invite participants to get their refreshments before the session begins. Don't use some of those valuable ninety minutes getting up for refreshments. (But a stand-up stretch break after an hour is always welcome.)

Equipment and Supplies

Each group member—not each couple—should have a copy of the study book to highlight, jot marginal notes in, and so on. Let group members know that the study book is theirs to keep; the days of keeping the study books clean of marks so that they can be put in the church library are over (thankfully!). Each group member should bring a Bible to each session. Which version? Any version that's best described as a translation, not a paraphrase will be useful, because a variety of translations enriches discussion! Have paper and pens and pencils available in case some have forgotten to bring these. A markerboard (or chalkboard) will be invaluable, as will a large pad of paper on an easel. Don't forget the markers in a variety of colors.

Of course, you'll want the television set or projection screen where everyone can see it easily for the video. You'll need to cue up the video component for each session in advance of the session. Nothing is more frustrating for study group members than the leader fiddling with the television set controls and the remote controls during the session. Refer to the "Prepare" section each lesson to see if you'll need to gather other supplies that aren't listed here.

Your Own Preparation

In a word, prayer! And more prayer! Pray for each participant in the group. Pray before reading each chapter. Pray upon completing the reading. Pray while reading the Bible passages. Pray while reading this leader guide. But keep in mind that the study book and the leader guide are not Scripture; only the Bible is. It's OK to disagree with the study book or the leader guide. It's OK to seek help in understanding the biblical passages and the study book ideas before the session. But remember: You are not the authority (and you don't have to be). You are not the arbiter of right and wrong ideas. It's OK if group members come out of a session with a variety of ideas! You are a learner with the group members. You facilitate the learning experience, but you are a full participant in the discussions. By and though your leadership, all the group members—including yourself—will grow in Christian faith and discipleship.

Session 1
The Gift of Good News

Key Scripture: Matthew 1:18-25

Overview

This session focuses on good news! How we all love to hear good news—but often we don't recognize news as good at the time. Do you think Joseph in our Scripture for today recognized the news the angel brought as good—or bewildering? And how about Mary (see Luke 1:26-38)? Was the angel's message to her perceived at the time as good news? How we wish the Gospel writers had included inflection or expression as they related these wonderful stories. Were Mary's words to the angel in verse 38 words of excitement? Resignation? fear? or what?

This session will explore how the news of the coming of Christmas can be both exciting and challenging. It will rely heavily on the study book *All I Want for Christmas,* on the DVD, on the Scriptures, and on the experiences of the group members.

As a result of participating in this session, group members should develop a renewed understanding of the good news of the coming of Christmas and recognize new ways to make that good news the good news in their lives.

Prepare

Here's a quick checklist to remind you how to prepare for this session (and every other one too):

❑ Did you distribute copies of the study book to all participants at least a week ahead of your first session, along with instructions to read the first chapter before your first meeting?

❑ Are the tables and chairs arranged ahead of time to facilitate discussion? Is the room comfortably warm or cool as the case may be?

❑ Is the markerboard or large paper in place where all can see it, with markers on hand?

❑ Are refreshments out and ready for early arrivals? Remember to encourage folks to get their refreshments as they arrive so you don't have to take a refreshment break midway through the session.

❑ Are the television set and DVD player (or computer and screen) in place for all to see? Is everything plugged in and remote control at the ready? (Extra batteries for the remote are always a good idea!)

❑ Are Bibles—perhaps several translations—available on the tables?

❑ Are paper and pencils or pens available?

❑ Are the "Starter Questions" prepared on index cards? Refer to the "Good News of Faith, Hope, and Love" section below to see what is needed.

❑ Are there enough small pieces of paper for everyone in the group? Refer to the "Close the Session" section below to see what is needed.

❑ Are you prepared early so you can greet folks as they arrive rather than scurrying around with last-minute details?

Welcome and Opening Prayer

Welcome folks as they arrive, invite them to the refreshments, and then encourage them to find chairs around the square of tables. Encourage spouses not to sit together.

Start promptly at the time announced, even if all expected participants are not present yet. Welcome the participants, and if necessary, ask each group member to introduce herself or himself. ("Table tent" name tags might be helpful for larger groups.)

You might begin with this prayer:

> Almighty God, as we enter this holy time of the year, we ask your presence with us as we seek to understand anew the wonderful gift of your Son. Make us aware of all we must do so that this Advent observance and the celebration of the coming Christmas might fill us with new understanding and an awareness of your presence with us. In all we are and all we do, let us hear again the good news of Advent and Christmas! We pray together in the name of the One who taught us this prayer:
>
> Our father, who art in heaven . . . (continue with the Lord's Prayer).

Open the Session

Ask the participants to divide into teams of three around the tables. Team members might draw their chairs together in order to hear more easily. (If necessary, one team might have two or four members so that all can participate.)

Direct each member of a team to describe briefly for her or his teammates a time when some incoming big news seemed frightening at first, but then became a blessing. Instruct teams to take no more than five minutes for team members to think about such a situation. Then encourage the participants to share their experiences within their teams. Don't rush this; give everyone time to think and recall; then allow team members to share their experiences within the teams. (Hint: Don't allow one or two persons to monopolize a team discussion; be sure each team member has adequate time to share.)

With participants still in their teams, ask one member of the group to read aloud Matthew 1:18-25 and another group member to read aloud Luke 1:26-38.

Ask each team to discuss how the experiences the team members heard from one another were similar to or different from the experiences of Joseph and Mary.

Now invite each team to appoint one member to share with the whole group the experience of another team member. What possibly frightening news became good news for that person? Note: Don't allow the team spokesperson to relate her or his own experience for the whole group. This will ensure that team members listen well to one another.

Allow a few minutes for comments and discussion by the whole group after each team has reported, but keep this general discussion brief.

Engage

Now prepare to show the video. Use a simple transition statement, such as, "Let's see what the video says about good news, even though the news may not seem so good at first." Keep your hand on the remote control for the DVD player, and remind the group members that they can ask to have a section of the video replayed for clarification or reinforcement. Encourage group members to speak up immediately and ask for a replay rather than waiting until the video is finished.

Play the video for Session 1 entitled "The Gift of Good News."

Ask the whole group a couple of open-ended questions after you all have viewed the video. You may choose from the questions below, or formulate others based on what stands out to you in the video:

- *What new insights into good news did you discover from viewing the video?*

- *Did the video give you any new understandings of good news? If so, explain briefly.*

- *How did the video clarify ideas contained in the study book?*

- *How are you inspired or challenged by the story of the toymakers at church?*

- *What is the relationship between the gift of God's presence and the gifts of faith, hope, and love?*

The Good News of Faith, Hope, and Love

Now move into a consideration of the three big ideas contained in Chapter 1 of *All I Want for Christmas*. You might ask the whole group to call out the three big issues as you write them on the large sheet of paper or markerboard. These three are the writer's contention that Advent and Christmas bring us the good news of faith, hope, and love.

Form three teams, each team to explore one of these big ideas. Ask the group members to count off around the tables by three, that is, one, two, three, one, two, and so on. The ones will form one team, the twos another team, and the threes a third team. Do not worry if one team has one or two fewer members than another team. (Note that "counting off" in this ways puts group members with a different cluster of group members than they were with during the initial activity. This enriches discussion and sharing and tends to prevent one or two persons from dominating the conversation.)

Ask the teams to form up by switching chairs and rearranging themselves. Each team should appoint a recorder, who will be a full participant in the team discussion but will also jot down notes on the team's ideas.

Give each team a set of "Starter Questions" to get their discussion started. Ideally, you will write these questions on 3-by-5 cards in advance of the session, and hand them out to the teams at this time. The Starter Questions for each team are listed below. Encourage the teams to use these to spark thought and conversation.

Team One will discuss the gift of faith. Here are their Starter Questions:

- *What is faith?*

- *How do the study book and the video define faith?*

- *How would you define faith so that a ten-year-old would understand what you mean?*

- *How does one "get" faith? How does one lose faith?*

- *What tests our faith?*

- *How does the Advent and Christmas experience enrich and perhaps redefine our faith?*

Team Two will discuss the gift of hope. Here are their Starter Questions:

- *What is hope?*

- *How do the study book and the video define hope?*

- *What is the Christian hope?*

- *How is Christian hope different from pie-in-the-sky wishing for something, such as, "I hope I get that new set of kitchenware for Christmas"?*

- *How do we deal with reality when hope is dashed? For instance, "I hoped he would recover from the illness, but he did not."*

- *Is Christian hope more than "I hope I get to heaven"? Explain your responses.*

And Team Three will discuss the gift of love. Here are their
Starter Questions:

- *What is love?*

- *How do the study book and the video define love?*

- *What causes us to gain love or lose love?*

- *How is the love that is a special gift at Advent and Christmas
  different from the "Be My Valentine" kind of love?*

- *How is this love alike and different from the love of wife and
  husband, or parent and child?*

- *What does the love we receive at Advent and Christmas
  demand of us?*

Reassemble as a whole group and ask for a report from each
team. The recorder may make this report, or it can be someone
else designated by the team. Each team member can and should
add to the report. Let all members of the group raise questions
of clarification or elaboration as needed. Then as a whole group,
discuss these questions:

- *How are faith, hope, and love related to one another?*

- *How do we experience all three at Advent and Christmas?*

- *What is unique about your individual experience of faith,
  hope, and love during Advent and Christmas? What is
  unique about our experience of these things together
  as a church?*

- *What does this experience expect from us as Christians in
  today's world?*

Close the Session

Distribute small pieces of paper, one to each group member. Invite each group member to jot down on that piece of paper one major learning or "take away" from this session that will enrich her or his observance of Advent and Christmas this year. Challenge group members to put that "take away" in his or her purse or wallet and refer to it often during this Advent season.

Invite the group members to pray silently for the kind of faith, hope, and love that are gifts of God's unlimited grace. Send everyone away with a blessing, looking forward to your meeting next week.

Session 2
The Gift of a New Understanding

Key Scripture: Luke 1:39-56

Overview

This session will help members of your study group remember. It will help them recall the ways they have viewed God; how they have seen others, especially strangers; and for what purposes they have been living. As a result of conversations and reflections during this session, group members should emerge with a new awareness of God, a new appreciation of others, and new and renewed insights into their own existence. A tall order? Yes! But that is what happens to and with us at Advent and Christmas: We take the risk of making radical changes in our lives because of a new recognition and understanding of what God has done—and is doing—for us in the Incarnation.

Prepare

Refer to the bulleted list of preparations in the Session Plan for the first session on pages 11–12. How did these arrangements work out at your first group meeting? "Tweak" these suggestions as necessary to fit your particular meeting space and accommodations.

In addition to the items on that list, have these other supplies ready for your group members as they arrive:

❑ Paper and writing instruments for each group member. Place one or two sheets of 8.5-by-11 paper or notebook paper and a pen or pencil on the table in front of each chair.

❑ Index cards. Place one or two 3-by-5 cards (or similar sized slips of paper) in front of each chair.
❑ Wrapping paper. Put a piece of Christmas wrapping paper on the table at each chair. These need be no larger than about 8 inches by 8 inches.

Hint for group leaders: Do the activities in this leader guide along with group members. You are a member of the group, a full participant. Do with the group members what you are asking them to do. If an activity calls for sharing, try to share with different group members.

Welcome and Opening Prayer

Complete your preparations well ahead of time so that you can greet participants as they arrive. Invite them to visit the snack table or to fill their snack plates from the containers on the tables before the session begins. Again, try to avoid a refreshment break in the middle of the session. A mid-session snack break destroys continuity and the logical development of the session in addition to requiring too much time.

Start your meeting on time, even if everyone has not yet arrived. When it's time to begin, welcome the whole group, then open the session with this or a similar prayer:

> Almighty and ever-loving God, you have promised to make all things new. Make new our understanding of you, of our sisters and brothers, and of ourselves during this Advent and Christmas season. Forgive us when we sometimes wish that this season would scurry by so that we can return to our regular routines. May the mystery and infinite joy of Christmas be born again in us this year. We pray in the name of Christ our Lord. Amen.

Open the Session

Read aloud Luke 1:39-56 in this way: Go around the tables, each person in turn reading a verse aloud until the passage has been read aloud by the whole group. Before the first person reads, encourage everyone to read in this way. Say:

> "Read with as much expression and inflection as you can; avoid at all costs reading in a monotone. Your interpretation of the inflection of a verse may not be the same as someone else's, but that's all right. The concern here is to express how you think Elizabeth spoke to Mary and how do you think Mary responded."

After you have read the passage aloud in this way, discuss any new insights or understandings of this passage you discovered based on hearing it read aloud with expression by several different voices.

Engage

Prepare to play the video. Remind the group members to call out "Stop" or "Replay" during the running of the video if someone wants to see or hear something on the video a second time for clarification. Stop and replay during the showing of the video; time will not permit replaying the entire video.

Ask for brief responses to the video, using the following questions as prompts:

- *How did the story about "Trash Trees" in the video demonstrate the gift of a new understanding?*

- *How can you learn to see familiar things through new eyes? What role does Jesus' coming play in helping you to do so?*

- *How did the video clarify ideas contained in the study book, especially the story of the other wise man?*

- *What new insights did you gain about your own understanding, and your need for a new understanding, through watching this video?*

A New Understanding of God

The book *All I Want for Christmas* reminds us that Christmas gives us a new picture of God. Invite each participant to take one of the 8.5-by-11 sheets of paper in front of him or her and to jot down her or his earliest understanding of God. Allow about five minutes for people to complete this exercise. Then invite them to complete this sentence in one or two words: "In my earliest memories of God, I thought God was . . ."

Next, ask the participants to form pairs, with each person working with the person sitting next to him or her. Instruct each pair to discuss their earliest recollections of what God is like, using the following questions:

- *How were these early ideas formed?*

- *What part did others play in forming these ideas?*

- *How often, if at all, did these early ideas about God change over the years? What made these changes come about?*

Ask each pair to join with another pair and discuss their responses to this question:

- *How does Christmas change our understanding of what God is like? Jesus as an adult showed us what God is like, yes, but how does the Christmas story demonstrate what God is like?*

(Keep in mind the shepherds, Joseph, Mary, the magi, and Simeon and Anna—all of the characters throughout the Gospels whom we associate with the birth of Jesus and its significance.)

Call everyone's attention back to the whole group and hear brief reports from each team of four. Ask each person to write on the piece of paper this sentence stem and complete it in as many words as necessary: "Christmas demonstrates for me that God is . . ."

A New Understanding of Others

The book *All I Want for Christmas* also shows how Advent and Christmas give us a new view of others. The author, James Moore, tells the moving story of Artaban, the other wise man, which we also saw in the video. Invite a group member to summarize the story of Artaban. Then discuss the following questions. (Note: If anyone is familiar with *The Story of the Other Wise Man*, you may wish to invite them to add elements from the story that the book and video did not include. This can enrich your discussion.)

- *What does The Story of the Other Wise Man tell us about the relationship between our understanding of God and our understanding of others?*

- *Why do we find it easier to develop renewed compassion and love for persons like us at Christmas than we do at other times?*

- *Why is it so hard to acknowledge that persons on the other side of the world, even those who practice different religions, are also our sisters and brothers and in need of our love and compassion?*

- *To pick up on the study book author, how do we see a reflection of God not only in people just like us but in our sisters and brothers who are Hindu, Buddhist, Muslim, or atheist?*

Ask each person to complete this sentence on his or her piece of paper: "Because of Advent and Christmas, I can now view others, all others, as . . ." Form groups of three, and invite everyone to share their sentence completions in these teams. Then bring the whole group back together, and ask each team to share (quickly) their responses with the rest of the group.

A New Understanding of Ourselves

Finally, *All I Want for Christmas* demonstrates that Christmas gives us a new understanding of ourselves, that is, a new and renewed purpose for living.

Refer to the study book and invite a group member to read aloud the first paragraph in the section "Christmas Gives Us a New Purpose for Living" on page 43.

Ask group members to take the sheet of paper in front of them and divide it roughly into thirds (vertically or horizontally). Everyone will need a blank sheet for this exercise; they can use the back of the sheet they've already written on, or they can get a new piece of paper.

At the top of the one third of the page, instruct them to write, "How I Share in the Christmas Story." At the top of the next third, instruct them to write, "How I Celebrate God's Love Daily." At the top of the last third, instruct them to write, "How I Pass God's Love On to Others." Ask each group member to complete each third of the piece of paper carefully and prayerfully by listing under each heading at least three specific ways that the "How" is answered. If group members have trouble describing how these three have been or are being accomplished, encourage them to come up with at least three ways they can begin to accomplish these goals. If time permits and group members are comfortable doing so, ask group members to cite some of their responses to the "How(s)," but do not push anyone to share who does not wish to do so.

Close the Session

Invite each person to take a 3-by-5 card and jot on that card at least one learning or insight from this session that will change the way she or he will respond to Christmas this year. Direct the group members to "wrap" this card in the piece of Christmas gift wrapping paper. They should plan to open this to recall what they have written on Christmas day.

Close with this prayer taken from the Christmas carol, "O Little Town of Bethlehem:"

> O Holy Child of Bethlehem,
> Descend to us, we pray;
> Cast out our, sin and enter in,
> Be born in us today.

Remind group members to read Chapter 3 in the study book before your next session. Although the listed Scripture for this next session is Joshua 24:14-15, invite group members to read Joshua 24 in its entirety before you meet again.

Session 3
The Gift of a Strong Foundation

Key Scripture: Joshua 24:14-15 (24:1-28)

Overview

This straightforward session deals with our sense of security and ultimate reality. To use another metaphor, it focuses on the basket in which we put all of our eggs. One of the significant learnings from this session is the recognition that each of us—whether consciously or not—has chosen what will be for us our absolute security. Thus, by the time the group has discussed several concepts at this session, each group member should acknowledge what for her or him is the ultimate thing on which he or she leans. A corollary is the question of how one can change one's sense of ultimate security, and, if so, how a person makes that change.

While the suggested Scripture for this session is two verses, group discussion will be enriched if participants are familiar with the entire twenty-fourth chapter of the Book of Joshua, or at a minimum Joshua 24:1-28.

Prepare

Again, refer to the bulleted list of preparations in the first session on pages 11–12, adjusting them as necessary for your group's specific needs. As always, make paper and pencils or pens available for all. You can enhance your own preparation by reading several commentaries on Joshua 24. The goal here is not to become deeply versed in the details of the biblical story, but rather to gain insight into the temptations that invited the Israelites to put their trust in false gods. These insights will help you to recognize the many ways we are tempted to put our ultimate trust in some of the false gods that surround us. Two commentaries you might wish to explore are:

- "The Book of Joshua: Introduction, Commentary, and Reflections," by Robert B. Coote, in *The New Interpreter's Bible* Volume II, edited by Leander E. Keck and others (Abingdon, 1998); pages 553–719.
- *Joshua*, by Jerome F. D. Creach, Interpretation Series (Westminster John Knox, 2003).

If possible, have copies of *The United Methodist Hymnal* available for group members. One copy for each two participants would be satisfactory.

Complete your preparations before participants begin to arrive. This way, you can greet and visit with each group member as she or he arrives. Don't forget to encourage participants to select their refreshments before the session begins. And, as always, begin—and end!—the session at the agreed upon time.

Hint for Group Leaders: Does the discussion sometimes get off track? Does a member (or several members) become fixated on a subject tangential to the discussion? Try suggesting this at the beginning of a session: Explain that if someone is off track in a discussion—including you!—one or more group members are invited to raise two fingers on a hand and gently raise and lower than hand quickly. The two fingers? Bunny ears! Why? Because someone is "chasing rabbits" rather than sticking with the subject! Do the bunny ears with good humor rather than malice, and group members will respond well.

Welcome and Opening Prayer

At the agreed upon starting time, call the group to order. Welcome them as a group, and quickly ask if any have special prayer concerns—praises or petitions. If so, include these in your opening prayer. The opening prayer may be something like this:

> Almighty and ever loving God, as we gather to consider your Word in and for our lives, we ask you to be present with us. Help us each to see you reflected in each member of this study group. And guide and direct our conversations at this time that we might each be brought closer to you. We pray in the name of your son, Christ Jesus. Amen.

Open the Session

Form teams of four persons. You might do this by "counting off" or simply by asking groups of four persons sitting together to be a team of four. Ask one person in each team of four to read and then paraphrase Joshua 24:1-4; ask a second person in each team to read and paraphrase Joshua 24:5-7; ask a third person in each team to read and paraphrase Joshua 24:8-10; and ask the fourth person in each team to read and paraphrase Joshua 24:11-13. Each team member should write his or her paraphrase on a piece of paper to share with the team. When each team member has completed his or her individual paraphrase, instruct each team to work together to paraphrase Joshua 24:14-15, and write it down.

What's a paraphrase? To "paraphrase a passage" is to put a passage into your own words, perhaps using contemporary words and phrases. It is to restate a biblical passage (in this case) into common English words.

Encourage group members to work quickly, then to share their paraphrases within their teams before the teams paraphrase Joshua 24:14-15.

Ask each team to share its paraphrase of Joshua 24:14-15 with the whole group, and if a few persons would like to share their paraphrases of the assigned passages from Joshua, allow them to do so. Raise these questions for discussion by the whole group:

- *How and in what ways are the Israelites Joshua addresses tempted to fail or fall short?*

- *What motivation does Joshua provide now for faithfully serving the Lord?*

- *What is at stake in the decision Joshua places before them?*

Engage

Before viewing the video, ask the whole group to brainstorm false gods to which people are attracted. You might ask two persons to write these down on a large sheet of paper or markerboard as they are called out. Participants may be slow getting started, but once group members catch the meaning of this exercise, they will keep the recorders busy. Pose this question for brief discussion by the whole group:

- *Where and how do persons learn about these false gods, these things people lean their weight on, only to find that they ultimately fail?*

Now view the video. As always, invite group members to interrupt the video by asking to have a brief section of it replayed for clarification and elaboration if needed. Discuss the following questions:

- *How do the River of Life and the Sellwood Faith Community serve as a strong foundation for their members? What evidence do you see of their strength?*

- *How do you respond to the uniqueness of these two expressions of church? What advantages do they have, and what drawbacks might they face?*

- *What new insights emerged for group members from the video and stories that were shared in it?*

- *What questions might you want to ask people of the River of Life or the Sellwood Faith Community?*

- *What foundations besides God are you tempted to lean your weight upon? What are some of the reasons why people choose to rely upon false gods?*

Ask group members to turn to Chapter 3 in the book *All I Want for Christmas*, and recall the three realities that the author says we can rely upon. (These are the strong foundations of family, church, and God.) List these on your large sheet of paper or markerboard.

Inspecting the Foundations

Now, form three teams (not necessarily the same teams that did the Bible paraphrasing earlier in this session). Assign one of these foundations to each team. Invite each team to discuss its assigned foundation with one another using open-ended questions such as these (you might choose to write these questions on the markerboard or large sheet of paper):

- *Is this foundation always reliable? Can you always count on this foundation? Give reasons and illustrations of your answer.*

- *What are some reasons why some folks may not perceive this foundation as always reliable?*

- *In what ways may some folks try to change this foundation before they are willing to lean upon it?*

- *What, if anything, does this foundation require or even demand of those who lean on it?*

- *What can you conclude about this foundation? Are you willing to lean entirely on this foundation? Why or why not?*

As you hear the teams' discussions winding down, gather the whole group back together. Hear a report from each team, and invite the listening teams to raise questions for clarification or to push the presenting team for a more complete explanation. Hint: Disagreeing with the presenting team is appropriate if the person disagreeing can support that disagreement with facts or examples.

Now raise this question for discussion by the whole group:

- *James Moore says that these three foundations, family, church, and God, are reliable. Can you think of other foundations that are completely reliable (especially if the group discovered that the family and the church are not always reliable in every way)?*

If a group member cites something as reliable, something you can lean your weight on, encourage the rest of the group members to raise questions, illustrations, or ideas that either support or challenge the group member who suggested this foundation.

As the group leader, you may summarize the discussion by suggesting that God and God alone is the only sure and absolutely reliable reality on which persons can lean completely. Raise these questions:

- *If God is thus reliable, why don't all persons lean completely on God and ignore the siren song of all the other realities clamoring for our allegiance?*

- *How do the facts that we cannot see God, we cannot be sure we hear God, and we are surrounded by so many ideas, theories, and beliefs about God fit into this discussion?*

• *Finally, what was Joshua's answer to all of this? How does his answer speak to us today?*

Close the Session

End your group's discussion by inviting the group to sing together "The Church's One Foundation," 545 in *The United Methodist Hymnal*. If your group is uncomfortable singing, you may choose to recite the words together instead.

Close with this or a similar prayer:

> God of glory and infinite love and grace, help us to grow in such faith and trust that we lean on you and you alone as the one unchangeable reality in our lives. But Lord, where our faith is weak, strengthen us. When doubts arise, reassure us. When fears assail us, protect us. "Lord, we believe; help our unbelief!" We pray in Christ's holy name. Amen.

Remind group members to read Chapter 4 of *All I Want for Christmas* before your next session. Adjourn on the time agreed to by the group members.

Session 4
The Gift of a New Style of Living

Key Scripture: Matthew 23:23-26

Overview

This may be a rather difficult session to lead for several reasons. Persons may be able and willing to change thoughts, ideas, and even beliefs, but this session calls for persons to change their style of living. It calls readers not just to change their style of living a little bit, but to change their style of living dramatically and drastically. This session focuses on committing one's self to living in a way that one's lifestyle is a consistent and constant reflection—not an occasional or one-time reflection—of a living faith in Jesus Christ.

Therefore, as a result of participating in this session, each group member should be able to take a serious census of herself or himself with this or a similar question in mind: "How do my actions, the way I live my life every day, and my attitude toward others reflect what I profess to be my Christian faith?"

In addition to the Scripture passages listed in the chapter, you may want to use Matthew 25:31-46 in several ways. It is used especially in the session closing activity.

Prepare

Again, use the bulleted list of preparatory steps contained in this Leader Guide for the first session on pages 11–12. This list is illustrative; you may want to add or delete steps or steps, supplies, and equipment depending on your group.

Because some of the activities in this Leader Guide for this session call for role playing, you may want to be sure that adequate space is available for the role plays and that all the group members can see and hear the "actors" in the roleplays.

Don't forget to have paper and pens or pencils on the tables, and place at least two different translations of the Bible on each table.

As always, be sure that you arrive at the meeting place in time to have all the preparations completed before the first participants arrive.

Welcome and Opening Prayer

Welcome the participants to this next-to-last session of *All I Want for Christmas*. You might remind the group members that as this study has progressed, the author's ideas and challenges have been more and more personal—that is, they are directed more and more specifically at the ways each of us lives her or his own life. In some ways, today's session is very personal; there will be little room for abstract discussions or conversations about specific Bible passages or arcane ideas. But remind group members that no one will be "put on the spot" or accused of not living up to his or her profession of faith. This is not a time for group judgment of individuals within the group, but a time for individual soul searching.

Open the session with this or a similar prayer:

> Lord of life, we gather to worship you and to learn
> from you the ways in which you call us to live. We
> are grievously aware of the ways our lives fail to
> reflect your love and of the deep difference between
> our words and our actions. Forgive us by your
> infinite grace and love, and equip us to make our

words and actions congruent with your perfect will
for us. We pray in Christ's holy name. Amen.

Open the Session

Ask each group member to take paper and a pen or pencil and
write the beginning of this question across the top of the page:
"What makes the way I live my life every day and in every
situation . . ." Then, down the left side of the page, write these three
words to complete the question, leaving space between the words.
The words are: "Compelling?, Contagious?, and Convincing?" (You
might diagram this a bit on the markerboard or large sheet of paper
so that all can arrange their pages the same way.)

Now ask group members prayerfully and carefully to write
down beside each of the three headings their first thoughts in
response to the three questions. Do not spend a lot of time on this,
but encourage each group member to write something for each of
the three words. Assure the group members that what they write
is for their eyes only; they will not be asked to share their written
responses with other group members or anyone else.

Engage

Direct the group members to the first sentence of the second
paragraph on page 101 of the book *All I Want for Christmas*. Ask
the group members to read this sentence aloud together. You might
write this sentence on the large paper or markerboard as they read
it aloud: "Christianity is not just a way of believing; it is also a way
of behaving." Ask the following questions for brief discussion by the
whole group:

- *Which comes first: believing or behaving?*

- *Can a person behave as a Christian without believing as a
  Christian? Give reasons and examples for your answer.*

Don't press the group for consensus; these questions have no clear and definitive answer.

Now show the video. As always, encourage group members to ask to have the video stopped so they can hear again a point or comment if they need clarification.

Form teams of three or four persons each. Instruct each team to discuss the video among themselves, identifying one main idea or story that stood out to them and one key question that they are left with after viewing the video. Ask each team to report on what they discussed, allowing the other teams to follow-up with questions or comments in response.

Compelling, Contagious, Convincing

With the group still in their teams, ask each team to discuss these questions (you might write these questions on the large paper or markerboard):

- *What does it mean to have a compelling faith?*

- *List examples from your own life of persons who had a compelling faith. What made their faith compelling?*

- *Now consider the other side: Have you ever known someone whose faith was less than compelling, even the opposite of compelling? What made this faith less than compelling?*

Give the teams several minutes to discuss these questions, but do not ask for reports from the teams at this time.

Now ask everyone to think silently about persons in their lives who have or had a contagious faith. Ask the group to consider these questions in silence:

- *Did you "catch" your Christian faith from someone? Who? How did this person make her or his faith contagious?*

- *In what ways? How did this person's life demonstrate the sentence from the study book that we read aloud and considered earlier?*

Ask each person in each team to describe briefly the person (or persons) whose contagious faith brought that team member closer to Christ. As a whole group, discuss briefly what common characteristics were shared by the persons the team members recognized as having a contagious faith.

Next, invite the teams to consider the third characteristic described by James Moore in his book: A faith that is convincing. Ask the following questions for discussion:

- *What does it mean to possess a convincing faith?*

- *Can a person have a compelling and a contagious faith without that faith being convincing? If so, how? (Hint: Think in terms of the "long term" here: A convincing faith is not a single example or illustration but a long term, perhaps life long, demonstration of faith in actions as well as words.)*

Again, give team members time to think of persons in their lives who had a convincing faith. Was that faith more apparent in words or in actions? If in actions, what were some of those actions? Share some examples of convincing faith.

Roleplay

Instruct each team to select one example of a compelling, contagious, or convincing faith to share with the whole group through a roleplay. Encourage each team to create a skit, involving every team member, that illustrates a compelling, contagious, or convincing faith. You may allow each team to choose which characteristic (compelling, contagious, or convincing) they will illustrate, or you may assign the characteristics to the teams.

Allow 5–10 minutes for the teams to plan their skits, and then gather the whole group back together to perform them.

When all the teams have shared their roleplay skits, ask the whole group to identify common characteristics of the persons or situations described. Again, call to mind that key sentence considered earlier in the session: "Christianity is not just a way of believing; it is also a way of behaving." Ask:

- *How can each of us come to live a faith that is compelling, contagious, and convincing?*

Close the Session

Ask each group member to reflect silently on this question:

- *How do my actions and my way of life reflect—or fail to reflect—what I claim as my beliefs?*

Earlier in the session, each group member was asked to write down ways in which his or her lifestyle was compelling, contagious, and convincing. Now ask each group member—for her or his eyes only!—to write prayerfully under each of those three headings how he or she could make his or her life and witness more compelling, more contagious, and more convincing. What changes in lifestyle would she or he have to make—want to make!—to match his or her belief with actions and habits?

Now ask a good reader to read aloud with feeling and expression Matthew 25:31-46. Pause for a few moments of silence at the conclusion of this reading, then offer this prayer to close your session:

> Almighty and ever-merciful God, we pray that our actions, our lives, our very being might always reflect your love for us. And may our actions and lives reflect our love for you through our love for others, whoever they might be. May our very beings reflect a compelling, contagious, and convincing

commitment to you as reflected in the ways in which we treat others. Make us instruments of your grace, your peace, and your love. We pray in the name of the one who taught us how to live, Christ Jesus our Lord. Amen.

Remind group members to read and be ready to discuss the fifth and last chapter of *All I Want for Christmas* before your next session.

Session 5
Christmas Gifts We Can Pass on to Others

Key Scripture: Matthew 2:1-12

Overview

This is your last session in this Advent study. But in this session (and book chapter), the tables are turned slightly as the focus is not on the gifts that Christmas can bring to us (if we are open and receptive), but on the special and unique gifts we can give to others. In several of the other sessions, James Moore emphasizes three dimensions of the unique gifts that Christmas brings to us. In this final chapter, the author lifts up five gifts that we can give and share with others, and we will explore each of those in the group session: the gift of time, the gift of kindness, the gift of appreciation, the gift of encouragement and the gift of love. Again, the study book writer offers five examples—but do not let the group limit its thinking to just these five.

Prepare

As always, refer to the bulleted list of steps on pages 11–12 in preparing to lead the session. Be sure the video player and the television screen are located where all can see, and be confident that everything is properly plugged in and operating—including being cued to this particular segment of the video.

For this session you will need easy access to the markerboard or a large paper, with markers, perhaps several different colors, on hand.

See the "Gifts We Can Pass on to Others" section below, and identify the four questions listed there. Write these questions on a separate large sheet of paper or on a section of the markerboard.

Spend some time thinking and praying about the close of this session and this study. How can you leave your fellow group members both inspired and challenged to view Christmas in a new way as a result of this study? And how can group members share that new view of Christmas with their families and friends—not so much in words as in actions?

As usual, complete all your preparations well ahead of your beginning time so that you can greet each participant as she or he arrives. Try to thank each participant for his or her contribution to this study.

Welcome and Opening Prayer

Welcome the group as a whole, and remind them that although this is the last session of this study, your prayer is that each group member will experience this study as the beginning of a new or renewed understanding of Christmas. You hope that each person will grow in understanding, experiencing, and sharing with family and friends this deeper meaning of the gifts that Christmas brings to us. Pray also that each group member will be made aware of the special gifts we can share with others, not just at Christmas but throughout the year.

Begin your session with this or a similar prayer:

Ever gracious and gift-giving God, be with us as we seek to comprehend the vastness of your love for us and as we seek to live in response to your infinite gifts by sharing those gifts with others. We praise you for the new insights gained through our study thus far. And we pray that we will continue to grow and experience the uniqueness of the Advent and Christmas celebration. We thank you for each member of this study group, and we pray that each of us will experience your presence, your grace, and your love. We ask all this in the name of Christ our Lord. Amen.

Open the Session

Ask participants to keep their study books closed as you begin with this activity. Say something like: "Over the past four weeks, we have talked about four special gifts that can be ours at Christmas. Please call out these gifts as I write them for us to see." Write the gifts on the large piece of paper or markerboard as your fellow group members call them out. (Note: These gifts need not be listed in order.)

Next, say: "James Moore has given us three examples of each of these gifts in the various chapters of *All I Want for Christmas*. Call out these three examples—and any additional examples that we raised in our discussions." As your group names these examples, write these down beside, underneath, or around the gifts you have already written. (Again, these examples need not be listed in order.)

Move now to today's session. Say: "In our chapter for today, the author gives us five examples of the special gifts 'that always fit' and that we can pass on this Christmas, every Christmas, and indeed every day. Let's list those five gifts that always fit and that we can give and share." Again, write these on the markerboard or paper as they are lifted up.

If the group is not able to list the four gifts given to us at Christmas along with the three examples of each and/or if the group cannot list the five special gifts "that always fit," encourage group members to open their study books and complete the outline on the large paper or markerboard. Pose this question for discussion by the whole group:

- *What significant insights about these gifts given to us at Christmas do we gain for our own lives from this outline—and from our recollections of our discussions?*

- *How do you feel God leading you to respond to what you have heard?*

Engage

Prepare to show the video (which you have previewed), again reminding group members that anyone can interrupt at any time to ask for a "rewind" in order to hear again a point for clarification or reinforcement. After viewing the video, discuss the following questions:

- *What new insights into the gifts that always fit do you gain from the video?*

- *How does the tradition of Las Posadas lift up the gifts of kindness and time?*

- *What do you think it means to those who receive hospitality through this tradition? What does it mean for those who give hospitality?*

- *How are these gifts different from the usual kinds of gifts we consider at Christmastime?*

- *Recall the mircoloan project from the video. Can you think of other creative ways to make gifts of encouragement and love a part of your regular Christmas gift-giving?*

Gifts We Can Pass on to Others

Form five teams. Assign each team one of the five "gifts that always fit" as described in the book, *All I Want for Christmas*. (These are: the gift of time, the gift of kindness, the gift of appreciation, the gift of encouragement, and the gift of love.) If you have a smaller group, assign to some teams two of the gifts. Challenge each team to discuss its assigned gift among themselves using questions such as these:

- *What is unique about this gift?*

- *What costs are involved in giving this gift? (Hint: Think beyond financial or monetary costs.)*

- *For whom is this gift most appropriate? Is this gift inappropriate for some? Give reasons for your answer.*

- *What are some reasons why it is sometimes difficult to give this gift? Or why is it difficult to give this gift to certain people?*

Next, ask each team member to describe a time in her or his life when he or she has been the grateful recipient of the assigned gift, and a time when she or he has given this gift to someone else. Ask:

- *What was the reaction of the recipient of your gift, and how did you respond upon receiving this gift from someone else? How did you feel upon receiving this gift?*

Call the teams back together into the main group, and hear a brief report from each team. Let the listening teams raise questions with the presenting team. What can the whole group conclude about gifts that always fit, which we can pass on to others?

More Gifts That Always Fit

Now as a whole group, brainstorm additional gifts that always fit that can be given at Christmas or at any other time. Write these down on your large piece of paper or markerboard as they are identified. As a gift added to the list, you may need to ask the contributor to explain the gift. For example, the gift of touch is appropriate in some places—many persons in nursing homes are seldom the recipients of loving touches. Or the gift of presence is an important contribution to another person in some situations. In these situations, words are inadequate, but "just being there" can be vitally important to a person in need. Invite group members to identify such gifts they have received, gifts that were non-tangible, unexpected, yet vitally important to the recipient at the time.

Call the group to a time of silent prayer, asking each member in silence to think of at least one person with whom the group member could give the gift of time, the gift of encouragement, the gift of kindness, the gift of appreciation, or the gift of love during this Advent and Christmas season.

What Have You Learned?

Finally, ask each group member to write down at least one significant insight that they have achieved from this Advent study. Encourage group members to write this idea or commitment in such a way that she or he can carry it in purse or wallet and refer to it often, not just at Christmastime, but throughout the coming year.

Close the Session

Because this is the last session of this study, ask group members to form pairs and share with each other what they have learned from this study. Then invite each person in these pairs to describe what she or he plans to do as a result of this study and what you all have learned from it. Ask one or more of the following questions to guide the discussion:

- *How will you change your observance of Christmas as a result of this study?*

- *What old ways of celebrating Christmas might you omit?*

- *What new celebrations of Christmas might you begin to recognize as ways to receive these four gifts of Christmas that God has provided through Christ?*

- *How will you share the unique gifts of Christmas with others throughout the year?*

Close with this or a similar prayer:

> Holy God of all, awaken our hearts and minds
> to your unique gift of Christ at this joyous time
> of the year. But awaken in us also the desire and
> determination to share the gift of Christ with
> everyone during this coming year. Make us
> instruments of your grace and peace, of your love
> and forgiveness, until every knee shall bow and
> every tongue confess that Jesus Christ is Lord.
> We pray in the name of the one who taught us to
> pray together: Our Father, Who art in Heaven . . .
> (continue with the Lord's Prayer).

As group members prepare to leave, thank each one for his or her contributions to the study.

Bonus: Organize a Churchwide Advent Study

*A*ll I Want for Christmas: Opening the Gifts of God's Grace leads readers to discover the gifts that Christmas has for us, and how we can experience those gifts through the miracle of God's presence in Jesus Christ. Resources for children, youth, and adults are available to facilitate a churchwide, intergenerational program on the basis of this book. Such a program provides opportunities for Christians of all ages to learn from one another, worship together, and celebrate the season of Advent through a shared experience.

Below, you will find a list of resources for the churchwide study; sample schedules for conducting the study as part of a weeknight program, Sunday school program, or weekend retreat; and ideas for the intergenerational gatherings.

Resources for the Churchwide Study

Adults

All I Want for Christmas: Opening the Gifts of God's Grace, by James W. Moore
All I Want for Christmas: Opening the Gifts of God's Grace Leader Guide, by John Gilbert
All I Want for Christmas: Opening the Gifts of God's Grace DVD

Youth

All I Want for Christmas: Opening the Gifts of God's Grace: An Advent Study for Youth, by Cindy Klick

Children

All I Want for Christmas: Opening the Gifts of God's Grace Children's Leader Guide, by Suzann Wade

Sample Schedule

Many churches have weeknight programs that include an evening meal followed by separate classes for children, youth, and adults. The following schedule provides one suggestion for organizing a weeknight program based on *All I Want for Christmas: Opening the Gifts of God's Grace.*

5:30 P.M.	Meal
6:00 P.M.	Intergenerational gathering introducing Bible passages and main ideas for the lesson. This time may include skits, music, and prayers.
6:30-7:45 P.M.	Classes for children, youth, and adults.

Churches may want to do the Advent study as a Sunday school program rather than a weeknight program. While this would be similar to a weeknight setting, the suggested schedule does not include a meal and meeting times are shortened to fit a normal Sunday school schedule.

10 minutes	Intergenerational gathering
45 minutes	Classes for children, youth, and adults

Churches may also choose to do the Advent study as a weekend retreat. This setting includes meals, worship, intergenerational gathering times, and classes for children, youth, and adults. The suggested schedule below allows for teaching of all the content in a condensed two-day time frame.

Friday

5:30-6:00 P.M.	Light dinner
6:00-6:30 P.M.	Worship
6:30-8:00 P.M.	Session 1 classes for children, youth, and adults

Saturday

8:30-9:30 A.M.	Worship
9:30-11:00 A.M.	Session 2 classes for children, youth, and adults
11:00-11:30 A.M.	Intergenerational gathering
11:30am-12:30 P.M.	Lunch
12:30-2:00 P.M.	Session 3 classes for children, youth, and adults
2:00-2:30 P.M.	Intergenerational gathering
2:30-4:00 P.M.	Session 4 classes for children, youth, and adults
4:00-5:30 P.M.	Session 5 classes for children, youth, and adults
5:30-6:00 P.M.	Closing worship

Choose a schedule that works best for your congregation and its existing Christian education programs. Adapt the suggested schedules above to fit your needs.

Ideas for Intergenerational Gathering

Worship

Lead a brief worship service each week, including lighting candles on an Advent wreath, reading Scripture, and singing hymns as a group. Be sure to invite children, youth, and adults to participate in leading the worship services, giving them opportunities to introduce the hymns, read the Scriptures, and light the candles. Below are short readings for each Advent candle, Scripture passages, and hymn suggestions for each week.

Supplies:

Advent wreath with four purple candles (or three purple and one pink) and 1 white candle in the center.

- Matches

- A Bible

- Copies of *The United Methodist Hymnal* (enough for each person to sing)

Preparation:

Identify and ask persons to light the Advent candles, read the Scriptures, and introduce the hymns. Set up the Advent wreath and candles in a central location, which will be the focal point for your worship services.

Week 1:

Light the Advent Candle:

Say: "The first Advent candle symbolizes Christ our hope. As we light it, we remember the good news that Jesus comes as Emmanuel, God with us. May this good news be a light of hope in our hearts."

Light one of the purple candles.

Read the Scripture:
Say: "A reading from the Gospel of Matthew, Chapter 1."
Read Matthew 1:18-25.
Say: "This is the Word of God for the people of God."
All respond: "Thanks be to God."

Sing the Hymn:
"O Come, O Come, Emmanuel" (the *Hymnal*, 211)

Week 2:

Light the Advent Candle:

Light one of the purple candles. Say: "The second Advent candle symbolizes love. As we light it, we remember how God changes our hearts and our minds, giving us the power to love. We see and know that God is love, and that by loving others we love God. May the light of love shine in our hearts and lives."

Light the second purple candle.

Read the Scripture:
Say: "A reading from the Gospel of Luke, Chapter 1."
Read Luke 1:39-56.
Say: "This is the Word of God for the people of God."
All respond: "Thanks be to God."

Sing the Hymn:
"Blessed Be the God of Israel" (the *Hymnal*, 209)

Week 3:

Light the Advent Candle:
Light two of the purple candles. Say: "The third Advent candle symbolizes joy. As we light it, we remember that our lives are built upon God, a sure foundation. When we lean on God and trust in God, we find reason to be joyful. May the light of joy be warm and bright within us."

Light the third purple candle (or the pink candle).

Read the Scripture:
Say: "A reading from the Book of Joshua, Chapter 24."
Read Joshua 24:14-15.
Say: "This is the Word of God for the people of God."
All respond: "Thanks be to God."

Sing the Hymn:
"The Church's One Foundation" (the *Hymnal*, 545)

Week 4:

Light the Advent Candle:
Light three of the purple candles (or two purple and one pink). Say: "The fourth Advent candle symbolizes peace. As we light it, we remember the new life of peace and love that Christ brings to us. It is our blessing to be peaceful people, following Christ the Prince of Peace. May the light of peace guide our relationships with those around us."

Light the fourth candle.

Read the Scripture:
Say: "A reading from the Gospel of Matthew, Chapter 23."
Read Matthew 23:23-26.
Say: "This is the Word of God for the people of God."
All respond: "Thanks be to God."

Sing the Hymn:
"I Want to Walk as a Child of the Light"" (the *Hymnal*, 206)

Week 5:

Light the Christ Candle:
Light all four candles on the outside of the Advent wreath. Say:
"The fifth candle is the Christ candle. As we light it, we remember
that Christ is with us. The gifts of good news, a new understanding,
a strong foundation, and a new way of living come to us because of
the greatest gift of all: the gift of God's Son. May Christ be our light
today and every day."

Light the Christ candle in the center of the wreath.

Read the Scripture:
Say: "A reading from the Gospel of Matthew, Chapter 2."
Read Matthew 2:1-12.
Say: "This is the Word of God for the people of God."
All respond: "Thanks be to God."

Sing the Hymn:
"Joy to the World" (the *Hymnal*, 246)

Make Paper Prayer Chains

Bring your church together in prayer by inviting all participants of *All I Want for Christmas* to make paper prayer chains.

Supplies:

- Multi-colored construction paper
- Markers
- Glue Sticks
- Scissors

Preparation:

Cut sheets of construction paper length-wise to make two-inch wide strips, which can be formed into circles to make individual chain links. Set up tables where people can sit together, and place the strips, markers, and glue sticks at the center of each table.

This is an intergenerational activity, so ideally each table will have a mix of adults, children, and youth. Families may choose to sit together so that they can talk about the people they lift up in prayer, but be sure that they conduct the activity and have conversations with others outside their family as well.

With everyone seated at the tables, instruct each person to write the names of people they wish to pray for on the strips of construction paper. Write one name per strip. See the guidelines below about the names to write and pray for each week. After the names have been written, begin forming the prayer chains. Form the first strip into a circle by gluing its ends together. Then thread the second strip through the first, and form it into a circle by gluing its ends together. Continue in this manner until all the names are part of the chain. Say a short prayer for each name as you add that person to the prayer chain.

When each individual's chain is finished, join the whole table's chains together to make one chain for the table. Then join all of the tables' chains together to make one large chain for the whole room. Stretch the chain along one wall, or form it in a circle around your gathering space. Say a short prayer as a group for everyone whose name is included in the prayer chain.

Week 1: Write the names at least three people who have shared the good news of Jesus with you, and at least three people who need to hear the good news of Jesus this Advent. Say a short prayer for each of these persons as you start making the chain with their names.

Week 2: Write the names of at least three people in whom you have met Jesus. Say a short prayer for each of these persons as you add their names to your prayer chain.

Week 3: Write the names of at least three people in your family or three people in your church (or three of each!) who have been a strong foundation for you, someone you could rely on and count on. Say a short prayer for each of these persons as you add their names to your prayer chain.

Week 4: Write the names of at least three people you have seen make their faith real by the way that they live it out. Say a short prayer for each of these persons as you add their names to your prayer chain.

Week 5: Review your prayer chain, recalling each of the names you have added and how you have prayed for them over the past several sessions. Say a short prayer of thanks for each person represented on your chain, and ask God to bless them with the special gifts of Christmas this year.

Keep the group prayer chain together, displayed along one wall or in a circle around your gathering space. Each week, add the new names to the existing group prayer chain, so that the chain grows larger throughout the course of your study. When you gather for your fifth session, use this time to allow participants to read through the whole prayer chain and recall the names you have lifted up.

Perform a Skit

The *All I Want for Christmas* Children's Leader Guide, by Suzann Wade contains a short skit for each session to introduce the Bible lessons. You may adapt the lesson plan for the children's sessions to allow you to perform the skits as part of your intergenerational gathering.

Supplies:

Copies of the skits from each session of *All I Want for Christmas* Children's Leader Guide.

Costumes and other props for volunteers to dress up as the people in the skits.

Preparation:

Invite a volunteer or volunteers to perform the skit for the week, and give them a copy of the pages from the Children's Leader Guide. Allow them time to change into the costume, and encourage them to perform the skit at the appropriate time.

Week 1:   A Carpenter's Dream (page 11)
Week 2:   Mary's Gift (page 24)
Week 3:   An Old Shepherd's Tale (page 40)

Week 4:   John 1:1-5, 10-18: A Christmas Story of Darkness
           and Light (page 56)
Week 5:   Follow the Star (page 66)

If you choose to do these skits as a part of your
intergenerational gathering time, the skits will best serve as a
transition to the separate classes for children, youth, and adults.

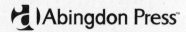

Everything you need to turn this book into
an all-church Advent study

Help your whole church explore the wisdom in popular author James W. Moore's *All I Want for Christmas*. The complete selection of resources is listed below. 5 sessions.

9781501824197. Adult Study Book
9781501824210. Adult Study Book Large Print
9781501824203. Adult Study eBook
9781501824227. Leader Guide
9781501824234. Leader Guide eBook
9781501824241. DVD
9781501824258. Youth Study Book
9781501824265. Youth Study eBook
9781501824272. Children's Leader Guide

Visit your local book retailer for details.

Abingdon Press™
Growing in Life, Serving in Faith